I WANT TO BE A LAWYER

Written by
Jonathan Reule

Illustration
Caballero Peza Mauricio
&
Caballero Peza Gabriel Fernando

Storyboard
Christiane Tee

First paperback edition May 2023
ISBN 978-981-18-6519-0

Published by Unibino Pte. Ltd.
31 Rochester Drive Level 3, #03-47 Singapore 138637

www.unibino.com

Have you ever been wrongly accused of doing something that someone else did? Or have you ever tried to tell the truth about an event only to find that nobody believed you? If that's so, then you might understand why it's so important to have lawyers in our modern society. You see, lawyers play a crucial role in our world by providing guidance and representation to those in need. Being a lawyer requires not only an understanding of the law but also the ability to think critically and navigate complex situations.

If you're interested in justice and enjoy solving problems, then a career in law might be right for you. Whether you're fighting for the rights of individuals, helping businesses navigate the legal system, or working on behalf of the government, a career as a lawyer can be both challenging and rewarding. Before delving deeper into what it takes to become a lawyer, let's have a glance at the history and evolution of this profession.

A struggle for survival characterised the early days of human existence, as we were not equipped with physical attributes such as large tusks or sharp teeth like many other creatures on the planet. Instead, we had to rely on our intellect to overcome challenges through the creation of tools and quick thinking in dangerous situations.

But as helpful as these attributes were, they still weren't enough to ensure our survival. We soon realised that we needed to rely on others. With more people around, the greater safety and security we had. However, these bigger communities also brought about different personalities and beliefs, which also brought about conflicts and disputes among us.

Understanding the need to resolve these issues without jeopardising our communities, we developed systems to organise ourselves and maintain order. Initially, we appointed village chiefs as the leaders of our communities. These individuals were tasked with resolving conflicts and addressing concerns among the members of our communities. The decisions made by the village chief were final and had to be respected by all members.

Yet as our communities expanded beyond mere villages and into entire kingdoms, we adopted a new system of leadership, mainly giving kings and queens authority to rule over our nations. This allowed for a more organised and centralised approach to governing, ensuring the smooth functioning of our societies and the protection of our citizens.

However, this system came with its own drawbacks and flaws. In particular, these chiefs, kings and queens were still humans with their own individual preferences. Often their decisions would rule in favour of those they favoured best, not who was genuinely guilty or innocent, for that matter.

The unequal distribution of resources and unfair treatment often experienced by common people caused frustration and anger. As a result, the demand for a fair and just system of governance grew. However, it would take several hundred years before such systems could be put in place, leaving people without adequate legal protection for an extended period of time.

This gradual shift led to the emergence of democratic systems, where every individual was given a voice and had the opportunity to express their views and opinions. This marked the start of a new era, where concepts like fairness and justice began to take hold, and people were no longer subject to the arbitrary decisions of a single leader.

But creating a democratic system is not as easy as it sounds. It requires a willing community to agree to these practices, along with a structured system that will take into account the majority of people's wishes. Today, most nations have come to an agreement on how democracies should be established. That is with legislative branches to formulate laws, law enforcement agencies that pursue criminals, and judiciary branches that ensure laws are followed properly.

Now, why don't we have a look at these different branches to understand our legal system better? The legislative branch is normally made up of a group of representatives who help create new laws and amend old or outdated ones. These representatives are chosen by the people through regular elections, ensuring that the diverse needs and views of the entire population are taken into account when creating new laws and modifying existing ones.

These elected representatives in the legislative branch of government engage in discussions, suggest new laws, and cast their votes on the proposed legislation. The process of creating or revising laws can be time-consuming as it requires thorough consideration of a wide range of perspectives and examination of extensive legal documents. Laws can cover a range of topics, from criminal activities like theft to traffic regulations like setting speed limits on roads.

These laws are then enforced by the police, who are trained professionals ready to assist citizens by investigating crimes, maintaining order, and, if necessary, making arrests. After apprehending potential criminals, the police will then send them to a court where they will undergo a trial to determine if they are innocent or guilty.

At this trial, people who are accused of doing something wrong will have to tell their side of the story and show any proof they may have to prove their innocence. At the same time, the person who says they were hurt or had something taken from them will also show proof to try to convince the judge that the accused person is guilty. This can sometimes become complicated, especially if one person is more knowledgeable about the law or if either of them is nervous about speaking in front of a judge.

This is why having a lawyer is so important in today's world. They are experts who step in to ensure that everyone gets a fair opportunity to present their case to the judge. With years of training and a deep understanding of the law, they can best protect their client's interests without letting any small detail fall through the cracks during their trials.

Lawyers help by presenting evidence and facts of each case in an organised and clear manner. They can also help advise their clients on their legal rights and obligations or even represent their clients in court and negotiate on their behalf if needed. In short, lawyers play a vital role in making sure that the justice system operates in a fair and impartial manner.

Of course, there are different types of lawyers, each of which specialises in a particular field of law. For instance, if you're planning on buying a new home, you may seek the assistance of a property lawyer to ensure that you are fully informed of all the details involved when purchasing your new home.

On the other hand, if you're getting married or going through a divorce, a family lawyer can help guide you through the legal process and represent you in court. Other common areas of law include criminal, business, and personal injury, and you would hire a lawyer who specialises in these fields for related cases. In this way, having the right lawyer on your side can provide peace of mind and a better outcome in any legal matter.

Just as there are various lawyers in the world, there are also various courts in which these lawyers work. Session courts, for instance, are primarily responsible for handling criminal cases. They determine the guilt or innocence of a defendant and pass a sentence accordingly.
On the other hand, High Courts are mainly concerned with appeals from session court cases, although they can take up serious criminal cases if needed.

Finally, the Supreme Court is the highest court of the land, tasked with interpreting laws and determining how they should be applied.

Unlike other courts, the Supreme Court takes up fewer trials but occasionally hears special appeals cases. But that doesn't mean their function is any less important, as they often deal with cases in which the decisions have a far-reaching impact on the entire legal system and the country as a whole.

If you're interested in becoming a lawyer, you may be wondering about the necessary education and skills. Generally, a bachelor's degree is required. While many aspiring lawyers choose to study pre-law, English, philosophy, or any major that develops your analytical and critical thinking abilities can be beneficial. It's important to select a degree program that will equip you with the skills you need to carefully interpret and analyse complex texts, as this is a critical component of legal education.

After earning a bachelor's degree in a relevant field, such as pre-law, English, or philosophy, the next step is to take the Law School Admission Test (LSAT). Law schools use this standardised test to assess applicants' reasoning, analytical, and critical thinking skills.

Upon completion of the LSAT, students can apply to law schools and earn their Juris Doctor (JD) degree. However, before becoming a licensed lawyer, candidates must pass the bar exam, which evaluates their knowledge of the law and ability to practise law professionally.

This process may seem long, but it's essential to become a skilled lawyer. Lawyers play a key role in modern society and must have a comprehensive understanding of the law to effectively assist and represent their clients in court. Being a lawyer is more than just winning cases - it's about advocating for the rights and interests of those seeking legal assistance.

Also, by being knowledgeable, articulate, good at listening and compassionate, lawyers are able to navigate the complex legal systems in place and bring about justice for those who would otherwise be marginalised or mistreated.

Whether it's through negotiating settlements, presenting arguments in court, or providing legal advice, lawyers have the power to shape our society and make a positive impact on the lives of individuals and communities.

In addition to providing legal representation in court, lawyers can also help keep companies safe by making sure their agreements and deals are legal and fair.
They can write up important documents and check over massive agreements before they are signed. By doing so, they help businesses make informed decisions and protect their long-term success.

Lawyers also play an important role in family law. They can help families navigate through the legal system and provide guidance on various matters, such as adoption or child custody matters. They work to ensure that the best decisions are made for all parties involved, taking into consideration each family's unique situation.

Intellectual property lawyers are a special type of lawyer who helps artists, writers, filmmakers, and companies protect their creative works, such as books, movies, music, and artwork.

These lawyers make sure that creative individuals' ideas and works are protected from being copied or used without permission. For example, if you were to create a movie about a cow-like monster made of bubble gum and named Sticky-Moo, you could talk to a lawyer to make sure nobody else makes a movie using your original character without your permission.

Sports lawyers specialise in providing legal assistance to athletes, sports teams, and leagues on various legal matters. They ensure that all parties comply with the rules and regulations, both on and off the field. For instance, a sports lawyer can assist a team that wants to change its name, logo, or uniform by handling the legal aspects of the process.
HAWKS
HAWKS
HAWKS
birds
birds
birds

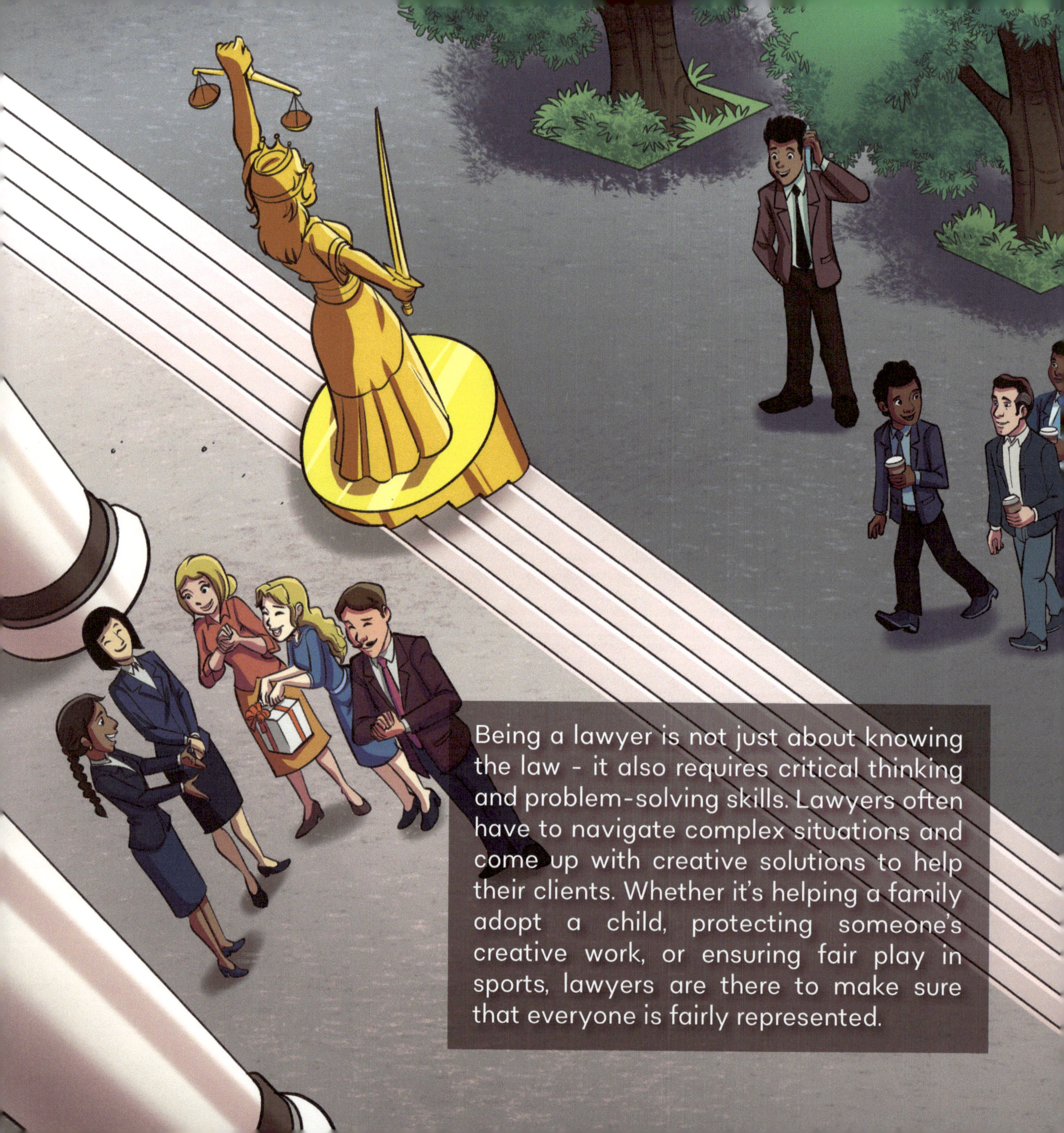

Being a lawyer is not just about knowing the law - it also requires critical thinking and problem-solving skills. Lawyers often have to navigate complex situations and come up with creative solutions to help their clients. Whether it's helping a family adopt a child, protecting someone's creative work, or ensuring fair play in sports, lawyers are there to make sure that everyone is fairly represented.

As you continue to learn and grow, you might find that being a lawyer allows you to make a real difference in the world. The possibilities are endless, and the skills you gain as a lawyer can be applied to many different fields and endeavours. But no matter what you choose, always remember to give it your best, and never limit your own future possibilities!

Shubhi Saxena
Founder, Unibino

My Inspiration

As a parent in this ever-changing world, it can sometimes feel overwhelming when it comes to our children's futures. New technologies seem to be arising almost every day, and with so many innovations, it creates unique professions which many of us wouldn't have dreamed to be necessary only a few years ago. Which to me is a good thing. Because with so much variety, my children can have the opportunity to pick a career that will fit their personalities and build upon their strengths. As you may imagine, this desire within me to provide my children with the resources they needed to thrive, led me to search out books that would be easy enough for them to understand while teaching them about various professions.

Only, I found that these books were few and far between. Even if I could find a book about a certain profession geared towards young readers, I found them sparse inside and limited to only certain careers that may not fit my children's abilities. This is when I came up with the idea to write my own children's books, teaching them about all the various careers in the modern world. After months of researching different professions and learning more than I ever expected, I quickly realised this was going to be a bigger project than I first anticipated. I dove into the histories of these professions, discovering links to the past, and why these professions were now so important.

Ultimately my goal was to offer my children options, to show them that there is no one set path for everyone. But in this, I stumbled upon something bigger. I wanted to share this with future generations. To share with all children and parents about these careers, to help spark curiosity, and to instil a passion for the future. Everyone has special talents and abilities, and I hope that this series will be able to offer clarity and inspiration to children around the world. Because at the end of the day, it's never too early to start dreaming and never too late to take action. With this, I hope you enjoy this series and that your young ones become the best versions of themselves as they can achieve.

www.ingramcontent.com/pod-product-compliance
Ingram Content Group UK Ltd.
Pitfield, Milton Keynes, MK11 3LW, UK
UKHW060101300726
14090UKWH00003B/345
* 9 7 8 9 8 1 1 8 6 5 1 9 0 *